Halloween Memory Book

A lifetime Halloween memory photo album to record Halloween celebrations every year

Page designer: Leda Vaneva

Spirala Publishing

Spirala Memories Journals

Spirala Publishing

Spirala Publishing
contact@spiralaPublishing.com
www.spiralaPublishing.com

Publisher's Note: This is a work of fiction. Names, characters, places, and incidents are a product of the author's imagination. Locales and public names are sometimes used for atmospheric purposes. Any resemblance to actual people, living or dead, or to businesses, companies, events, institutions, or locales is completely coincidental.

Ordering Information:
Quantity sales. Special discounts are available on quantity purchases by corporations, associations, and others. For details, contact the "Special Sales Department" at the address above.

Spirala Journals / Halloween memory book: A lifetime Halloween memory photo album to record Halloween celebrations every year - 1st ed.

Distributed by:
Speedy Publishing LLC
40 E. Main St. #1156
Newark, DE 19711
www.speedypublishing.co

Introduction

Greetings from all of us at Spirala Publishing! We would like to congratulate you on your interest in the Spirala Memories Journals collection for chronicling your life's precious memories.

Spirala Memories Journals is a specially-crafted series of journals, designed to accompany your family through life's memories. The object of each journal is to help the owner record the special events and occasions through the years, serving as a memory book to help you keep your fondest memories close to your heart.

Special events and occasions and their record as memories is what strengthens family bonds. These memories form a lasting impression that can be cherished, as well as helping one feel the warmth of home. Hence, keeping memories alive by recording them in a memory journal can be a great holiday gift and a treasured tradition for you and the people close to you. Your children will appreciate these memories for years to come.

Recorded memories can serve as a keepsake for your children or anyone you've given these journals as a gift. Keeping memory journals is something that your children can teach their future children about when they are grown, as a part of your family tradition. The journals can also be something that you can share with other special people in your life.

These days, we are so bombarded with information and are so busy with everyday life, that it can be easy to forget just how special quality time and holidays spent with loved ones truly are. Days and events can just blur together and get lost in time. We at Spirala Publishing understand that people like you love these special memories and need some help in keeping a record of them. And so the Spirala Memories Journals collection was born.

Spirala Memories Journals were created with you in mind. Each journal page is designed to be aesthetically pleasing and easy to use.

 Each memory book is dedicated to one celebration or holiday. Each book has a page to write your memories and another page to paste a photo of that occasion.

As these journals give another meaning to events that occur during the years by making them extra notable, you can make writing in these journals a special family tradition, effectively establishing the foundations of new family traditions which your children and their children will love.

Imagine having a memory book that you can show to you grandchildren: one that will keep your family stories alive and allow you to easily hand them down to future generations. This is a great gift for your children, and one that will stay with them forever, letting them feel the warmth of home wherever they are in the future.

Would you love to have a record of loving memories that you can look at and share with people who are dear to you? Then start keeping journals that preserve and highlight your memories at their very best. Start with yourself so you can share your beautiful memories later. After all, memories become more special when you show how much you value them.

ENJOY!

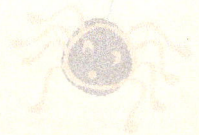

Date: _____

Favorite Traditions:

_____

Additions to Old Traditions:

_____

Costumes Worn:

_____

Favorite Tricks:

_____

Favorite Treats:

_____

Holiday Movies We Enjoyed:

_____

Parties/Special Events:

_____

Comments:

_____

Place for
your photo

Date:

Favorite Traditions:

Additions to Old Traditions:

Costumes Worn:

Favorite Tricks:

Favorite Treats:

Holiday Movies We Enjoyed:

Parties/Special Events:

Comments:

Place for
your photo

Date: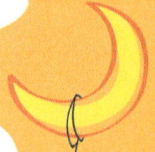

Favorite Traditions:

Additions to Old Traditions:

Costumes Worn:

Favorite Tricks:

Favorite Treats:

Holiday Movies We Enjoyed:

Parties/Special Events:

Comments:

Place for

your photo

Date: _____

Favorite Traditions:

_____

Additions to Old Traditions:

_____

Costumes Worn:

_____

Favorite Tricks:

_____

Favorite Treats:

_____

Holiday Movies We Enjoyed:

_____

Parties/Special Events:

_____

Comments:

Place for

your photo

Date:

Favorite Traditions:

Additions to Old Traditions:

Costumes Worn:

Favorite Tricks:

Favorite Treats:

Holiday Movies We Enjoyed:

Parties/Special Events:

Comments:

Place for
your photo

Date:

Favorite Traditions:

Additions to Old Traditions:

Costumes Worn:

Favorite Tricks:

Favorite Treats:

Holiday Movies We Enjoyed:

Parties/Special Events:

Comments:

Place for

your photo

Date: _____

Favorite Traditions:
_____

Additions to Old Traditions:
_____

Costumes Worn:
_____

Favorite Tricks:
_____

Favorite Treats:
_____

Holiday Movies We Enjoyed:
_____

Parties/Special Events:
_____

Comments:
_____

Place for
your photo

Date: _____

Favorite Traditions:

_____

Additions to Old Traditions:

_____

Costumes Worn:

_____

Favorite Tricks:

_____

Favorite Treats:

_____

Holiday Movies We Enjoyed:

_____

Parties/Special Events:

_____

Comments:

_____

Place for
your photo

Date:

Favorite Traditions:

Additions to Old Traditions:

Costumes Worn:

Favorite Tricks:

Favorite Treats:

Holiday Movies We Enjoyed:

Parties/Special Events:

Comments:

Place for

your photo

Date:

Favorite Traditions:

Additions to Old Traditions:

Costumes Worn:

Favorite Tricks:

Favorite Treats:

Holiday Movies We Enjoyed:

Parties/Special Events:

Comments:

Place for
your photo

Date: _____

Favorite Traditions:

_____

Additions to Old Traditions:

_____

Costumes Worn:

_____

Favorite Tricks:

_____

Favorite Treats:

_____

Holiday Movies We Enjoyed:

_____

Parties/Special Events:

_____

Comments:

_____

Place for

your photo

Date:

Favorite Traditions:

Additions to Old Traditions:

Costumes Worn:

Favorite Tricks:

Favorite Treats:

Holiday Movies We Enjoyed:

Parties/Special Events:

Comments:

Place for

your photo

Date:

Favorite Traditions:

Additions to Old Traditions:

Costumes Worn:

Favorite Tricks:

Favorite Treats:

Holiday Movies We Enjoyed:

Parties/Special Events:

Comments:

Place for
your photo

Date: _____

Favorite Traditions:

_____

Additions to Old Traditions:

_____

Costumes Worn:

_____

Favorite Tricks:

_____

Favorite Treats:

_____

Holiday Movies We Enjoyed:

_____

Parties/Special Events:

_____

Comments:

_____

Place for

your photo

Date:

Favorite Traditions:

Additions to Old Traditions:

Costumes Worn:

Favorite Tricks:

Favorite Treats:

Holiday Movies We Enjoyed:

Parties/Special Events:

Comments:

Place for

your photo

Date:

Favorite Traditions:

Additions to Old Traditions:

Costumes Worn:

Favorite Tricks:

Favorite Treats:

Holiday Movies We Enjoyed:

Parties/Special Events:

Comments:

Place for
your photo

Date: _____

Favorite Traditions:

Additions to Old Traditions:

Costumes Worn:

Favorite Tricks:

Favorite Treats:

Holiday Movies We Enjoyed:

Parties/Special Events:

Comments:

Place for
your photo

Date:

Favorite Traditions:

Additions to Old Traditions:

Costumes Worn:

Favorite Tricks:

Favorite Treats:

Holiday Movies We Enjoyed:

Parties/Special Events:

Comments:

Place for

your photo

Date:

Favorite Traditions:

Additions to Old Traditions:

Costumes Worn:

Favorite Tricks:

Favorite Treats:

Holiday Movies We Enjoyed:

Parties/Special Events:

Comments:

Place for
your photo

Date:

Favorite Traditions:

Additions to Old Traditions:

Costumes Worn:

Favorite Tricks:

Favorite Treats:

Holiday Movies We Enjoyed:

Parties/Special Events:

Comments:

Place for

your photo

Date:

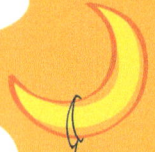

Favorite Traditions:

Additions to Old Traditions:

Costumes Worn:

Favorite Tricks:

Favorite Treats:

Holiday Movies We Enjoyed:

Parties/Special Events:

Comments:

Place for
your photo

Date: _____

Favorite Traditions:

_____

Additions to Old Traditions:

_____

Costumes Worn:

_____

Favorite Tricks:

_____

Favorite Treats:

_____

Holiday Movies We Enjoyed:

_____

Parties/Special Events:

_____

Comments:

_____

Place for
your photo

Date:

Favorite Traditions:

Additions to Old Traditions:

Costumes Worn:

Favorite Tricks:

Favorite Treats:

Holiday Movies We Enjoyed:

Parties/Special Events:

Comments:

Place for
your photo

Date:
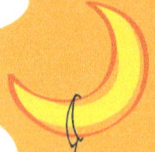

Favorite Traditions:

Additions to Old Traditions:

Costumes Worn:

Favorite Tricks:

Favorite Treats:

Holiday Movies We Enjoyed:

Parties/Special Events:

Comments:

Place for
your photo

Date:

Favorite Traditions:

Additions to Old Traditions:

Costumes Worn:

Favorite Tricks:

Favorite Treats:

Holiday Movies We Enjoyed:

Parties/Special Events:

Comments:

Place for
your photo

Date:

Favorite Traditions:

Additions to Old Traditions:

Costumes Worn:

Favorite Tricks:

Favorite Treats:

Holiday Movies We Enjoyed:

Parties/Special Events:

Comments:

Place for
your photo

Date:

Favorite Traditions:

Additions to Old Traditions:

Costumes Worn:

Favorite Tricks:

Favorite Treats:

Holiday Movies We Enjoyed:

Parties/Special Events:

Comments:

Place for
your photo

Date:

Favorite Traditions:

Additions to Old Traditions:

Costumes Worn:

Favorite Tricks:

Favorite Treats:

Holiday Movies We Enjoyed:

Parties/Special Events:

Comments:

Place for

your photo

Date:

Favorite Traditions:

Additions to Old Traditions:

Costumes Worn:

Favorite Tricks:

Favorite Treats:

Holiday Movies We Enjoyed:

Parties/Special Events:

Comments:

Place for
your photo

Date:

Favorite Traditions:

Additions to Old Traditions:

Costumes Worn:

Favorite Tricks:

Favorite Treats:

Holiday Movies We Enjoyed:

Parties/Special Events:

Comments:

Place for

your photo

Date:

Favorite Traditions:

Additions to Old Traditions:

Costumes Worn:

Favorite Tricks:

Favorite Treats:

Holiday Movies We Enjoyed:

Parties/Special Events:

Comments:

Place for
your photo

Date:

Favorite Traditions:

Additions to Old Traditions:

Costumes Worn:

Favorite Tricks:

Favorite Treats:

Holiday Movies We Enjoyed:

Parties/Special Events:

Comments:

Place for

your photo

Date:

Favorite Traditions:

Additions to Old Traditions:

Costumes Worn:

Favorite Tricks:

Favorite Treats:

Holiday Movies We Enjoyed:

Parties/Special Events:

Comments:

Place for
your photo

Date:

Favorite Traditions:

Additions to Old Traditions:

Costumes Worn:

Favorite Tricks:

Favorite Treats:

Holiday Movies We Enjoyed:

Parties/Special Events:

Comments:

Place for
your photo

Date:

Favorite Traditions:

Additions to Old Traditions:

Costumes Worn:

Favorite Tricks:

Favorite Treats:

Holiday Movies We Enjoyed:

Parties/Special Events:

Comments:

Place for

your photo

Date:

Favorite Traditions:

Additions to Old Traditions:

Costumes Worn:

Favorite Tricks:

Favorite Treats:

Holiday Movies We Enjoyed:

Parties/Special Events:

Comments:

Place for

your photo

Date:

Favorite Traditions:

Additions to Old Traditions:

Costumes Worn:

Favorite Tricks:

Favorite Treats:

Holiday Movies We Enjoyed:

Parties/Special Events:

Comments:

Place for
your photo

Date:

Favorite Traditions:

Additions to Old Traditions:

Costumes Worn:

Favorite Tricks:

Favorite Treats:

Holiday Movies We Enjoyed:

Parties/Special Events:

Comments:

Place for
your photo

Date:

Favorite Traditions:

Additions to Old Traditions:

Costumes Worn:

Favorite Tricks:

Favorite Treats:

Holiday Movies We Enjoyed:

Parties/Special Events:

Comments:

Place for

your photo

Date:

Favorite Traditions:

Additions to Old Traditions:

Costumes Worn:

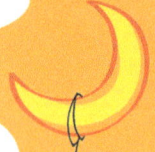

Favorite Tricks:

Favorite Treats:

Holiday Movies We Enjoyed:

Parties/Special Events:

Comments:

Place for

your photo

Date: _____

Favorite Traditions:

_____

Additions to Old Traditions:

_____

Costumes Worn:

_____

Favorite Tricks:

_____

Favorite Treats:

_____

Holiday Movies We Enjoyed:

_____

Parties/Special Events:

_____

Comments:

_____

Place for
your photo

Date:

Favorite Traditions:

Additions to Old Traditions:

Costumes Worn:

Favorite Tricks:

Favorite Treats:

Holiday Movies We Enjoyed:

Parties/Special Events:

Comments:

Place for
your photo

Date:

Favorite Traditions:

Additions to Old Traditions:

Costumes Worn:

Favorite Tricks:

Favorite Treats:

Holiday Movies We Enjoyed:

Parties/Special Events:

Comments:

Place for
your photo

Date:

Favorite Traditions:

Additions to Old Traditions:

Costumes Worn:

Favorite Tricks:

Favorite Treats:

Holiday Movies We Enjoyed:

Parties/Special Events:

Comments:

Place for
your photo

Date:

Favorite Traditions:

Additions to Old Traditions:

Costumes Worn:

Favorite Tricks:

Favorite Treats:

Holiday Movies We Enjoyed:

Parties/Special Events:

Comments:

Place for
your photo

Date: _____

Favorite Traditions:

Additions to Old Traditions:

Costumes Worn:

Favorite Tricks:

Favorite Treats:

Holiday Movies We Enjoyed:

Parties/Special Events:

Comments:

Place for

your photo

Date:

Favorite Traditions:

Additions to Old Traditions:

Costumes Worn:

Favorite Tricks:

Favorite Treats:

Holiday Movies We Enjoyed:

Parties/Special Events:

Comments:

Place for
your photo

Date:

Favorite Traditions:

Additions to Old Traditions:

Costumes Worn:

Favorite Tricks:

Favorite Treats:

Holiday Movies We Enjoyed:

Parties/Special Events:

Comments:

Place for
your photo

Date:

Favorite Traditions:

Additions to Old Traditions:

Costumes Worn:

Favorite Tricks:

Favorite Treats:

Holiday Movies We Enjoyed:

Parties/Special Events:

Comments:

Place for

your photo

Date:

Favorite Traditions:

Additions to Old Traditions:

Costumes Worn:

Favorite Tricks:

Favorite Treats:

Holiday Movies We Enjoyed:

Parties/Special Events:

Comments:

Place for
your photo

Spirala Memories Journals Collection

The Holiday Memory Book

A lifetime Holiday journal to record holiday celebrations every year

Spirala Memories Journals

4th of July Memory Book

A lifetime Independence Day journal to record your 4th of July celebrations every year

Spirala Memories Journals

Thanksgiving Memory Book

A lifetime Thanksgiving memoir journal to record Thanksgiving celebrations every year

Spirala Memories Journals

TRAVEL MEMORY BOOK

A travel diary and travel photo albums for recording your sweet vacation moments

Spirala Memories Journals

Halloween Memory Book

A lifetime Halloween memory photo album to record halloween celebrations every year

Spirala Memories Journals

Christmas Memory Book

A lifetime Christmas memoir journal to record Christmas celebrations every year

Spirala Memories Journals

Birthday Memory Book

a LIFETIME MEMORY BOOK TO RECORD BIRTHDAY CELEBRATIONS every year

Spirala Memories Journals

Mother's Day Memory Book

A lifetime mother's day journal to record your special motherhood moments every year

Spirala Memories Journals

New Year Keepsake Journal

A memory book to record your New Year's celebration and resolutions

Spirala Memories Journals

Easter Memory Book

A lifetime Easter journal to record Easter celebrations & Easter egg hunt every year

Spirala Memories Journals

Father Memory Book

A lifetime memory book to record birthday celebrations every year

Spirala Memories Journals

Memorable Moments Journal

A memory book to record your special moments

Spirala Memories Journals

Visit our website to purchase more journals from this collection.

www.SpiralaPublishing.com/SpiralaMemories

Spirala Publishing

Cutting Edge Products with Quality Built In

Be the first to know about new products and other events.
Sign up to receive the Spirala Publishing Newsletter
via your E-mail address.

www.SpiralaPublishing.com/signup

CPSIA information can be obtained
at www.ICGtesting.com
Printed in the USA
LVHW062236150321
681644LV00032B/579